Land of Plenty

By Suzanne Weyn
Illustrated by Eric Reese

Scott Foresman
is an imprint of

Glenview, Illinois • Boston, Massachusetts • Chandler, Arizona •
Upper Saddle River, New Jersey

Illustrations
Eric Reese.

ISBN 13: 978-0-328-52526-3
ISBN 10:   0-328-52526-X

16 V0FL 18 17 16 15

Table of Contents

CHAPTER 1

CHAPTER 2

CHAPTER 3

CHAPTER 4

Dearest Colleen,

I am so glad your family is finally coming to New York. We have been here for six months, and it is so exciting. To tell the truth, I'm still not used to all the noise and tall buildings. It is very different from Galway. Maybe it's a little like Dublin, since Dublin is Ireland's biggest city, but I have never been to Dublin, so I don't know for sure. My address in New York City is on the envelope. Have Patrick write to me as soon as you arrive, and I will come find you.

Your true friend,
Maureen

Colleen O'Mara folded her friend's letter. She slipped it into the pocket of her ankle-length skirt. She didn't know how to read because she had never been to school. But her big brother, Patrick, who could read, had read it to her so often that she knew what it said. She was impressed that Maureen had been able to learn to read and write in the free schools of America.

The health inspector had given the go-ahead for people to leave the ship. The crowd that had made the long journey from Ireland to New York City was finally promenading down the steamer's gangplank. Colleen could hardly believe it. The long trip from Ireland had been hard, but they were finally in New York City.

It was 1880. Colleen thought that was a nice even year—a good time to start a new life in America.

Colleen held the hand of three-year-old Fiona, her sister. Fiona looked up at Colleen. Her eyes were round, amazed at the sights of New York Harbor. Her curls floated like a cloud around her face. "We here?" she asked.

Colleen ruffled Fiona's hair. She looked at the big ships and tall buildings. "Yes, we are. This is our new home."

With her other hand, Colleen gripped a battered suitcase. It contained two skirts; a soft, flannel nightgown; some underwear; two faded blouses; a horsehair brush; and a frilly blue satin ribbon. Colleen narrowed her blue eyes against the fierce sunlight. The strong ocean breezes flung her reddish hair into her eyes. Setting down the suitcase, she brushed the hair aside. Just in front of Colleen, her parents and two older brothers carried their belongings.

Colleen's father, Sean O'Mara, looked back over his shoulder at her. "Be careful of that suitcase, my girl," he advised. "It contains everything you own. You don't want to lose it."

Her father was flanked by his two sons, 16-year-old Patrick and 13-year-old Liam. Their mother, Maeve O'Mara, was just a few paces ahead.

"It doesn't matter if she loses that old case," said Liam. "She can just get a new substitute. We're in America now. America is the land of plenty."

CHAPTER 2 *The Land of Plenty*

Colleen smiled. Her father had said it so many times on the trip over: *America is the land of plenty.* In Ireland, they had farmed a small piece of land that they rented from a landowner. This last year the family's potato crop had not been good. As a result, money had been very tight. That's why they had come to America—the land of plenty.

"The land of plenty," Colleen repeated. "How many times have we heard *that*?" she said to her brothers.

"Only a hundred," Patrick answered, a smile in his eyes. He wore a tweed cap over his nearly black hair. At the bottom of the gangplank, Patrick set down the large box he carried. It contained all the family's household belongings.

"He's said it a *thousand* times!" Liam piped up. He had the same red hair as Colleen, and the same vivid blue eyes. They sparkled with mischief now. "I'm sure Da has said it *exactly* one thousand times."

"Yes, I believe you're right, Liam," Colleen agreed with a grin. "*Land of plenty*, I agree—I *have* heard that phrase *exactly* a thousand times."

"So what if I *have* said it that many times," their father said with a good-natured smile. "It's the truth."

"And so it is!" Colleen's mother said. She held a handwoven, willow basket against her hip. "But getting all the plenty will take a lot of hard work. No one is going to hand it to us."

"Come on. That's enough resting," said Sean O'Mara. Colleen picked up her suitcase and squeezed Fiona's hand. Together, they moved forward with the crowd.

As they went, Colleen gazed at the other passengers who streamed from the ship. They were all tired from the long, cramped trip. They dragged trunks and baskets containing all they owned. Colleen looked at them with pride, despite their tattered appearance. In her eyes, they were brave, bold seekers of a better life. They were ready to take on whatever unfamiliar challenges America would confront them with.

CHAPTER 3 *Obstacles*

Colleen gripped Fiona's hand tighter. She didn't want to lose the little girl in the crowd. The people were heading for the Castle Garden immigrant processing center. It was at the bottom tip of New York City, right there beside the harbor. The center had been a fort against the British back during the War of 1812.

Two wide rivers ran on both sides of Castle Garden, the Hudson River on the west side and the East River on the east side. The rivers met in front of Castle Garden. They both flowed into the Atlantic Ocean at that spot.

Looking down the East River, Colleen saw two gigantic stone columns rising out of the water. Cables hung between them. "What's that?" Colleen asked Patrick.

Patrick O'Mara had learned to read from a friend, and he liked to read the newspapers. He was the only child in the family who knew how to read and write.

Patrick tipped back his cap and put his hands on his hips. "Would you look at that!" he said in amazement.

"What is it?" Colleen repeated her question.

"That must be the Brooklyn Bridge," Patrick said. "That's Brooklyn on the other side of the river. They started building that bridge ten years ago, and it's not finished yet. Look, men are high up there working. When it's done, it will be the longest suspension bridge in the world and one of the tallest structures in the western hemisphere."

Colleen smiled at her brother with pride. He was the brainy one in the family.

Patrick shook his head in wonderment. "I read all about it, though I never thought I'd ever see it. There it is—and I've only been in America for less than a half hour. That's plenty enough for me!"

The crowd moved closer to the Castle Garden building, and the O'Maras moved with it. Colleen could no longer see the amazing bridge. They went past the tall fence around the building. Castle Garden had a very wide entryway. A sign above the fence said, "For Immigrants Only." An American flag flapped in the wind. There was also a flag with the crest of New York State.

They joined the crowd of people moving inside to the great, round center room. It had a very high, domed ceiling. "My goodness," Colleen muttered, awed at the sight of the massive room. Even the church back in Galway was nothing like this!

The O'Maras got in one of the many lines. They crept forward slowly. Finally, they reached a desk where a uniformed official sat. He had a big ledger in front of him. He appeared to be writing information in the large book.

Along with her father, mother, and brothers, Colleen signed her name in the book. She was happy that they didn't ask her to write anything else. That would have presented a predicament. Her name was all she knew how to write.

Colleen's father produced a letter from their local country doctor back home. It said that the family was free of disease—not even a sprained wrist or ankle. Mr. O'Mara had made sure to get this letter before they left Ireland.

Mr. O'Mara had gotten the letter because he'd heard far too many stories of others who'd endured the grueling sea passage only to be turned back for reasons of ill health once they reached New York. Colleen was glad he'd thought of it.

"Address?" barked the official behind the desk, without looking up from the papers he was filling out.

Sean O'Mara suddenly looked nervous. The family had planned to find an apartment once they arrived. They didn't have an apartment yet, which meant they had no address.

The official looked up, annoyed. "Don't you have an address?" he asked. "We have to know where you'll be or you can't come in. You have to give an address where you'll be living in this country."

The O'Maras looked at one another, fear in their eyes. Would they be sent back to Ireland? They had come such a long way! The trip had been so long and hard! How could they send them back when they had come so far?

CHAPTER 4 *Quick Thinking*

"I need an address," the official said impatiently.

Colleen suddenly remembered Maureen's letter and came up with an ingenious idea. Colleen quickly pulled the letter from her pocket and handed it to her father. "Here's the address, Da," she said. "Here's where we will be staying, with Cousin Maureen."

Her father's face lit with understanding. "Oh yes, *Cousin* Maureen. Right. Yes. That's where we'll be staying." He read the address to the official. "One hundred Baxter Street."

"Very well." The official wrote down the address and then handed Mr. O'Mara a cardboard billfold of entry papers.

With a nod, Mr. O'Mara motioned his family to move away from the desk with him. They followed him a few paces until he stopped and faced them. "We did it! We made it through inspection!" he exulted, beaming with a triumphant smile. "Fast thinking, Colleen. That's my girl!"

"Thanks, Da," Colleen replied, feeling proud.

"Where to now?" Mrs. O'Mara asked.

"On to Baxter Street," he told them. "It sounds like a good place to start looking for an apartment. At least we have friends there. Let's be off. Our fortunes await us!"

Colleen stepped out onto the New York street a little nervous, but as thrilled as a Dalmation puppy to be in America. "I hear they have free schools in America," she said, turning to her parents. "I'd like to go."

"One as quick-witted and smart as you should definitely go to school," her father agreed. "I told you America is the land of plenty, didn't I?"

Castle Garden Immigration Center

When immigrants from other countries came to America between the years 1855 and 1890, they did not stop at Ellis Island. During those years Castle Garden was their first stop. It sat at the end of New York City in Battery Park.

Castle Garden had been built as a fort to defend against British attack during the War of 1812. Its location in New York Harbor between two rivers and facing the Atlantic Ocean made it perfect for defending against arriving war ships.

More than eight million immigrants from many different countries entered the United States through Castle Garden. Today it is run by the National Park Service and is part of the National Park Service of New York Harbor.

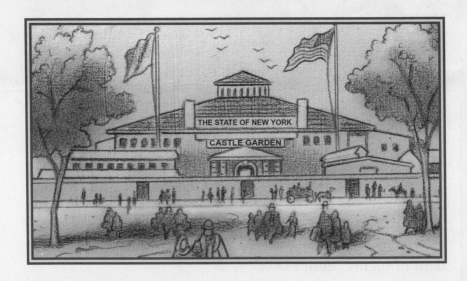